Helping Is...

by Jane Buerger and Jennie Davis
illustrated by
Kathryn Hutton

Published by The Dandelion House
A Division of The Child's World

for distribution by VICTOR
BOOKS a division of SP Publications, Inc.
WHEATON, ILLINOIS 60187

Offices also in
Whitby, Ontario, Canada
Amersham-on-the-Hill, Bucks, England

Published by The Dandelion House, A Division of The Child's World, Inc.
© 1984 SP Publications, Inc. All rights reserved. Printed in U.S.A.

A Book for Preschoolers.

Library of Congress Cataloging in Publication Data

Buerger, Jane, 1922-
    Helping is—.

    Summary: Explains the importance of caring for
other people, and suggests ways of being helpful to
family members, friends, and others.
    1. Caring—Moral and ethical aspects—Juvenile liter-
ature.   2. Helping behavior—Moral and ethical aspects—
Juvenile literature.   [1. Helpfulness.   2. Christian
life]   I.   II. Hutton, Kathryn, ill.
III. Title.
BJ1475.B84   1984   241'.4   84-7042
ISBN 0-89693-218-4

1 2 3 4 5 6 7 8 9 10 11 12 R 90 89 88 87 86 85 84

Helping Is...

Helping means caring for others . . .
like when my little sister is
sick and I stay inside to play
with her—even though my friends are
jumping rope just outside my window.

When my little sister is pulling her
wagon up the hill, and I push from
behind, that's helping!

And helping is holding a friend up
when he is learning to skate.

Helping is saying the "Thank-You"
prayer at dinner . . .

and holding Baby Brother on my lap
when Mom reads a Bible story.

When Baby Brother is sleeping,
helping is tiptoeing by his door.

Helping is wiping up spilled milk.

Helping is picking up my clothes
and putting them in the hamper.

Helping is washing my hands after making mud pies.

When the bird bath is dry, helping
is filling it with water.

Helping is taking care of my kitty.
It's feeding her and giving her fresh
water. It's also brushing her fur.

When Dad washes the car, helping is
rubbing it 'til it shines.

When company is coming for dinner,
helping is folding the napkins—very
carefully.

When our neighbors are away on
vacation and it hasn't rained,
helping is watering their roses.

Helping is doing hard things cheer-
fully—such as going to the doctor
or dentist.

Being helpful means caring about others. It's bringing food to church for the Thanksgiving basket . . .

or taking dinner to a neighbor who
is sick.

Helping is shoveling snow off the
front walk, so no one will slip. . .

and then wiping the snow off my
boots before going inside.

Helping is passing out the bells
at music time.

When teacher says, "Let's put up the
Christmas manger scene," helping is
waiting my turn. . . then putting my
piece in place—very carefully.

And later, helping is holding up Little
Sister so she can see it too!

Helping is telling a friend
about Jesus.

Helping is caring for one
another every day.

Care for One Another

Betty A. Riley